A Taste of culture

Foods of Morocco

Barbara Sheen

KIDHAVEN PRESS

A part of Gale, Cengage Learning

GALE
CENGAGE Learning™

Detroit • New York • San Francisco • New Haven, Conn • Waterville, Maine • London

© 2011 Gale, Cengage Learning

Every effort has been made to trace the owners of copyrighted material.

LIBRARY OF CONGRESS CATALOGING-IN-PUBLICATION DATA

Sheen, Barbara.
  Foods of Morocco / By Barbara Sheen.
    p. cm. -- (A taste of culture)
  Includes bibliographical references and index.
  ISBN 978-0-7377-5865-8 (hardcover)
  1. Cooking, Moroccan--Juvenile literature. 2. Morocco--Social life and customs--Juvenile literature. I. Title.
  TX725.5.M8S55 2011
  641.5964--dc22
                                                                    2010053852

Kidhaven Press
27500 Drake Rd.
Farmington Hills MI 48331

ISBN-13: 978-0-7377-5865-8
ISBN-10: 0-7377-5865-1

Printed in the United States of America
1 2 3 4 5 6 7 15 14 13 12 11

Printed by Bang Printing, Brainerd, MN, 1st Ptg., 05/2011

Contents

Bright Colors, Enticing Aromas, and Unique Flavors

The Kingdom of Morocco is located on the northwest tip of Africa, not far from Europe. It is a colorful and diverse country, famous for its fine food. Moroccans use a variety of ingredients in their cooking, but herbs and spices, dried and preserved fruits, bread, and olives are the ingredients Moroccan cooks cannot do without. They add the bright colors, enticing aromas, and delicate flavors that characterize Moroccan cooking.

More Prized Than Jewels

Since ancient times, Moroccans have been using spices and herbs to enhance their cooking without making

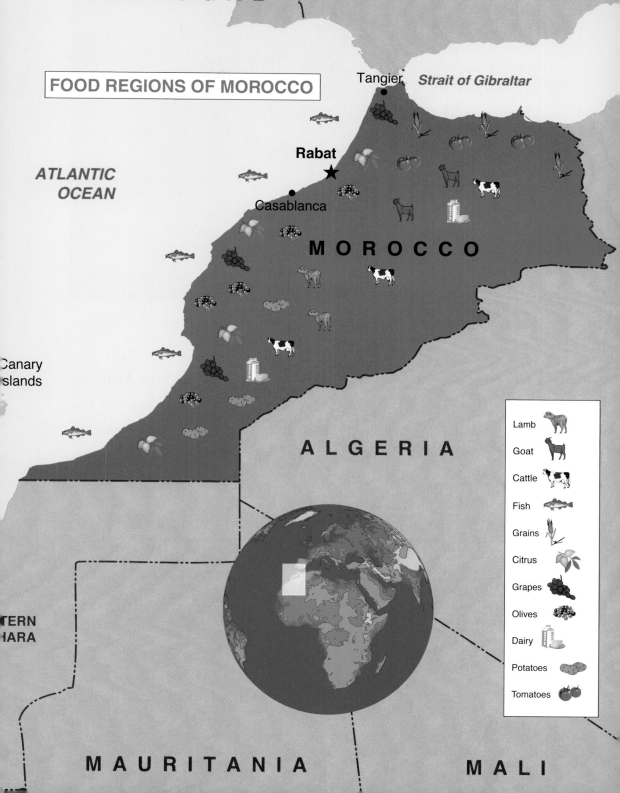

FOOD REGIONS OF MOROCCO

PORTUGAL

SPAIN

Tangier   *Strait of Gibraltar*

Rabat

ATLANTIC
OCEAN

Casablanca

M O R O C C O

Canary
Islands

ALGERIA

TERN
HARA

MAURITANIA

MALI

Lamb

Goat

Cattle

Fish

Grains

Citrus

Grapes

Olives

Dairy

Potatoes

Tomatoes

An outdoor market in Marrakesh, Morocco, where a variety of items, from spices to clothing, are sold.

the dishes overly hot and spicy. Phoenician traders passing through Morocco on ancient spice routes introduced Moroccan cooks to spices. Centuries later, Arabian invaders, who prized spices more than jewels, added to the Moroccan people's knowledge of how to use spices.

Modern Moroccan cooks have more than two hundred different herbs and spices to choose from. Spice stalls in Moroccan open-air markets, or souks (sooks), overflow with baskets, jars, tins, and sacks full of brightly colored herbs and spices. Their scents perfume the air. "Powerful aromas emanate from the mounds of red, gold, and brown powders, curious looking roots, bits of bark, shriveled pods, berries, bulbs, rose buds,

About Morocco

Morocco is located in North Africa just across the Strait of Gibraltar from Spain. It borders the Atlantic Ocean, the Mediterranean Sea, the nation of Algeria, and the territory of the Western Sahara.

Morocco has a mild climate and a diverse landscape, which includes two mountain ranges, the Sahara Desert, long coastlines, and fertile plains. Morocco also has many large cities. Rabat is the capital and the seat of government.

Morocco is a constitutional monarchy. A king and an elected parliament, or congress, rule the nation. Arabic is the national language. Many Moroccans also speak French.

Moroccan children are required to go to school until they are fifteen years old. But the law is not strictly enforced. More boys than girls attend school, especially in rural areas. The literacy rates for Moroccan males stands at 66 percent, as compared to 40 percent for females.

and orange blossoms, which are on display in the spice shops,"[1] explains author Claudia Roden.

Some of the most popular spices and herbs such as cinnamon, ginger, black pepper, mint, and parsley are familiar to North Americans. Others such as sweet-smelling orange blossoms, which Moroccans use to scent pastries and desserts, and yellow saffron are less familiar. Saffron has a slightly bitter taste. A little goes a long way, which is important because it is the most expensive spice in the world. A pound (0.45 kg) can cost anywhere from $600 to $2,000, depending on the quality.

A Perfect Blend

Moroccans rub herbs and spices on meat and fish, and they add them to stews, soups, salads, breads, desserts, and beverages. Most Moroccan dishes contain a variety of spices. For a dish to be considered well-cooked, no single spice should ever overpower the others. Instead, there must be a balance of flavors with each dish having its own distinctive taste, color, and perfume. In fact, Moroccans say that they can tell what their neighbors are cooking by the aroma of the spices drifting out of their kitchens.

Spices dominate Moroccan cooking, and each vendor has their own blend.

Moroccans rarely measure spices. Instead, they taste and smell whatever they are cooking to achieve the right balance. They use different spice mixtures for different dishes. The most popular of all Moroccan spice blends is called **ras el hanout** (raz-al-han-oot), which means "the shopkeepers choice." It contains anywhere from ten to one hundred different spices; although the average is twenty-five. Each spice vendor has his or her own secret blend. No two are alike, and every cook has a favorite.

Soft Crusty Bread

Spices are also used to scent and flavor Moroccan bread, which is served with every meal. Bread is a symbol of generosity and hospitality in Morocco, and is treated with respect. In fact, according to tradition, if a piece of bread is found on the ground, the finder is supposed to pick it up and put it somewhere safe, so it will not be stepped on.

Moroccan bread is sometimes described as flat bread similar to Middle Eastern pita bread. In reality, it is not actually flat. It is thick, disk-shaped, and slightly puffy with a chewy texture and a soft crust. Its shape and texture make it perfect for sopping up sauces and scooping up morsels of food. Because Moroccans eat with their fingers rather than with utensils, Moroccan bread serves as both a fork and a spoon.

The bread is usually made with a mixture of whole-wheat flour and coarsely ground bits of wheat, known as **semolina.** Sesame and **anise** seeds are often sprin-

Moroccan women selling their bread on the streets of Safi. Some bake their own bread in outdoor ovens while others choose to buy it from local sellers.

kled in the dough. The sesame seeds give the bread crunch. The anise seeds add a licorice-like flavor to the bread, which is baked fresh every day.

In rural areas, where many Moroccans do not own ovens, cooks prepare the dough every morning. They make a mark in it with a wooden stamp to show who the dough belongs to. Then, they send it to a large out-door wood-fired public oven to be baked.

It is a common sight to see children wearing pad-ded caps, carrying the bread on trays balanced on their heads. Author Catherine Hanger describes the sight: "Children collect the bread on their way home from school, and the sight of happy kids skipping home with loaves wrapped in brightly colored tea towels will provide some of your most enduring memories of Morocco."[2]

Other Moroccans have their own small outdoor ovens just for bread baking. For those people who are

Souks

Moroccan souks are ancient marketplaces filled with little shops and stalls laid out over miles of narrow twisting alleys and streets. Although the arrangement may appear to be haphazard, different street blocks are dedicated to different products. Among these products are spices, fruits, vegetables, meat, fish, baked goods, clothing, perfumes, jewelry, leather goods, tapestries, rugs, and handmade brass items, to name just a few. Most souks also contain dozens of little restaurants. Everything that is sold in a souk is clearly labeled with a price, but bargaining is a common practice.

Cars and other motor vehicles are not allowed in the souks, but donkeys are. Many souks are located behind a large public square, which serves as a gathering place for street entertainers who perform for people entering the souk. Musicians, sword swallowers, dancers, acrobats, and snake charmers are popular acts.

Moroccan souks are open-air markets where vendors sell a variety of products—spices, fruits, vegetables, meat, fish, baked goods, clothing, perfumes, jewelry, leather goods, tapestries, and rugs.

too busy to make their own bread, hot fresh bread is sold by street vendors, in bakeries, and in souks, where loaves are stacked in bins covered with brightly colored cone-shaped wicker, leather, or copper lids.

Sweet and Salty Fruits

Fresh bread goes well with dried fruits such as raisins, prunes, apricots, and dates, which are another essential element of Moroccan cooking. Moroccans like to mix sweet, salty, and savory flavors, and are as likely to add dried fruits to meat dishes and stews as they are to desserts. Dates, in particular, are especially popular. Thirty different varieties of this small sweet reddish

Lemons are preserved by pickling them in vinegar and salt for a month. They add tasty, unique flavor to many Moroccan dishes.

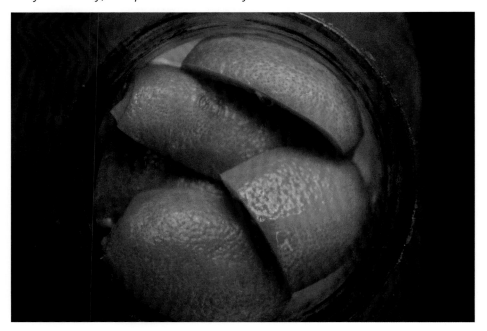

Moroccan Lemon Cake

Moroccans like the flavor of lemons. This is a simple light cake. The top can be sprinkled with powdered sugar.

Ingredients
2 cups flour
1¼ cup sugar
4 eggs
½ cup milk
juice of 1 large lemon
½ cup vegetable oil
4 teaspoons baking powder
pinch of salt

Instructions
1. Preheat the oven to 350 degrees.
2. Mix together flour, salt, sugar, and baking powder. Stir in the eggs, milk, and lemon juice. The batter should be smooth.
3. Spray a bundt or cake pan with non-stick spray. Pour the batter into the pan. Bake until a fork poked into the middle of the cake comes away clean, about 45 minutes. Let the cake cool before eating.

Makes one cake. Serves 10–12.

brown fruit grow in Morocco. Fish stuffed with dates is a favorite dish.

Dried fruit is also a popular dessert and snack. A bowl of dried fruit sitting in the center of a Moroccan table is a common sight. Dried fruit is also served to guests with tea. Preserved fruit, too, is very popular.

Fruit is preserved by pickling it in vinegar or brine, a salty liquid. Preserved lemons are a special favorite. To preserve the fruit, whole lemons are packed in salt and lemon juice for a month. During this time, the lemons soften and develop a slightly salty lemony flavor that is not as acidic, sharp, or sour as fresh lemons or as salty as pickles. They add a unique flavor to salads, stews, and chicken dishes. The lemons, according to author Paula Wolfret, are "one of the indispensable ingredients in Moroccan cooking...Their unique pickled taste and special silken texture cannot be duplicated."[3]

Many Colored Olives

Olives add another layer of flavor and color to Moroccan foods. Olive groves have been part of the Moroccan landscape ever since ancient Roman invaders planted olive trees throughout North Africa more than two thousand years ago. Today Morocco produces more than 400,000 tons of olives per year.

Big and small, smooth and wrinkled, green, violet, deep purple, and black olives are a colorful sight in Moroccan souks. "To experience the extraordinary variety of olives and their preparations, you need to stroll through the souq of any large town," Hanger explains. "Olives are heaped in every color and size, and flavored with a wide range of condiments such as paprika, chilli, cumin, coriander, and salt."[4]

All olives start out green and darken as they mature. Freshly picked olives are bitter and tough. They must be cured or preserved in salt and oil before they

Olive groves have been part of the Moroccan landscape for over two thousand years, and are eaten as appetizers or added to main dishes.

can be eaten. Moroccans add spices and herbs, such as cumin, garlic, and parsley, and juices, such as bitter orange juice, to the curing substances to scent and flavor the olives. Each type of olive has a distinct taste and use. Salty green olives are turned into olive oil. They are eaten in salads and are cooked with chicken and preserved lemons. A bowl of meaty black olives makes a popular appetizer. Moroccan stews would not

Olives and Chickpeas

This dish makes a good appetizer, side dish, or snack. It can be served chilled or at room temperature.

Ingredients
1 can (16 ounces) chickpeas, cooked, drained, and cooled to room temperature
1 cup cherry tomatoes
⅓ cup black olives, pitted
1 tablespoon fresh mint
3 tablespoons extra virgin olive oil
1 teaspoon lemon juice
½ teaspoon garlic powder
salt and pepper to taste

Instructions
1. Mix together the olive oil, lemon juice, garlic, salt, and pepper.
2. Put the chickpeas, tomatoes, olives, and mint in a bowl.
3. Pour the olive oil mixture over the chickpea mixture. Toss lightly.

Serves 4.

be the same without violet olives. They are a part of the distinct blend of colors, flavors, and aromas that make Moroccan cooking delicious and unique. Like the country itself, Moroccan cooks' favorite ingredients—olives, herbs and spices, dried and preserved fruit, and soft crusty bread—are vibrant and exciting.

A Cultural Blend

Morocco is an ancient land with a long history. Its first settlers were nomadic, or roaming, African people known as the Berbers. They arrived in Morocco about 2000 B.C. In the seventh century, Arabian armies trying to spread the Muslim religion to North Africa invaded Morocco in several waves. In 685 the Arabs took control of Morocco. The Arabs also took control of Spain, where they intermarried with the Spanish, creating a group known as the **Moors.** For centuries there was a close connection between the Moors and the people of Morocco. In fact, when the Moors were expelled from Spain in the 13th century, they settled in Morocco.

The Berbers were the first settlers in Morocco and their traditional hillside housing still exists in the country today.

In 1904 France took control of almost all of Morocco. Morocco did not gain its independence until 1956. All these groups helped shape Moroccan history and culture. Moroccan cooking reflects the influence of these different people. Favorite dishes such as **couscous** (coos-coos), **tagines** (ta-jeans), **bastilla** (bah-stella), and salads are signs of this cultural blend.

A Grain and a Dish

Couscous, which originated with the Berbers, is Morocco's national dish. The name refers to tiny granules of semolina similar to pasta and to any number of thick sauces that are served over the grain.

Couscous takes time, energy, and skill to prepare. First, cooks rub the couscous with flour, oil, and water until each grain has separated and started to swell. Then, they put it in a special pot called a **couscoussier** (coos-coos-ser). It has two sections—a pot with holes in the bottom and a larger pot in which the first pot sits. The grain is cooked in the smaller pot while the sauce is cooked in the larger. Fragrant steam from the sauce cooks, scents, and flavors the couscous without the grain coming in contact with any liquid that would make it soggy.

It takes about forty-five minutes to cook the grain. During this time, the cook removes the couscous from the steamer pot three times, and rubs it with more flour, oil, and water to remove any lumps. The couscous is not

Eating in Morocco

Moroccans eat three meals a day, with lunch being the main meal. Most businesses and schools shut down for lunch so that workers and students can go home to eat.

Moroccans eat seated on plush cushions and couches around a low round table. Traditionally, the women serve the men but eat separately from them, especially when male guests are present.

Moroccans eat with the fingers of their right hand. Their left hand, which is used for personal hygiene, is never used. Damp warm towels are passed around before and after the meal to ensure everybody's hands are clean.

The food is placed in the center of the table for all to share. Bread is passed around. It is used to scoop up food.

Easy Sweet and Spicy Couscous

This recipe uses instant couscous, which is sold in most supermarkets. It makes a good side dish. Stews and sauces can be poured on top of it. Water may be substituted for chicken broth. Dried cranberries or chopped dried apricots can be used in place of raisins.

Ingredients
1 cup instant couscous
1½ cups chicken broth
1 tablespoon butter
½ cup raisins
¼ cup slivered almonds
¼ teaspoon tumeric
1 teaspoon cinnamon

Instructions
1. Put the broth, butter, and spices in a saucepan and bring to a boil. Add the couscous, cover, and remove from the heat immediately. Let stand about 10 minutes or until liquid is absorbed.
2. Add the almonds and raisins to the couscous. Mix gently.
Serves 4.

done until each grain is separate, plump, and light.

Originally, the Berbers topped couscous with butter. Arab cooks added sauces containing chickpeas, vegetables, dried fruit, meat, and spices. Today there are probably as many different varieties of toppings as there are Moroccan cooks. With the exception of pork, which is rarely eaten in Morocco for religious

Couscous is Morocco's national dish and is served with a variety of sauces.

reasons, the combinations are limited only by the cook's imagination. Couscous with lamb, onions, almonds, and raisins is just one version. Couscous with seven vegetables and seven spices is another. Seven is considered a blessed number in Morocco, so this dish is especially popular on Friday, which is the Muslim Sabbath, or the seventh day.

No matter the variety, the grain and sauce are served as one dish, usually on a glistening brass tray. The grain is arranged in a pyramid with a hollow in the top into which the sauce is poured. To eat it, diners roll bits of couscous into a ball, dip the ball in the sauce, and pop it in their mouths, a practice that takes some skill. "The popping motion is important, because if performed inaccurately, the ball will crumble before it makes it into your mouth,"[5] explains Moroccan chef Lahcen Beqqi.

Sweet and Savory Stews

It takes less skill to eat Moroccan stews or tagines, which are famous throughout the world. Like couscous, tagines were originally a Berber dish that changed over time to reflect the influence of the different cultures that shaped Morocco. And, like couscous, the word tagine has two meanings—a special cooking pot and a wide range of slowly cooked stews that are made within it.

A waiter opens a tagine at a Moroccan restaurant. The shape of the tagine retains heat and traps steam, which keeps what is being cooked inside the pots from drying out, most commonly a stew.

Chicken Tagine

Here is an easy way to make a Moroccan tagine in a slow cooker.

Ingredients
2 pounds boneless, skinless chicken, cut in chunks
1 large onion, sliced
4 large carrots, peeled and cut in chunks
1 can (14 ounces) chicken broth
¼ cup tomato paste
1 teaspoon minced garlic
½ cup raisins
½ cup dried apricots, chopped
2 tablespoons flour
1 teaspoon each ginger, cumin, cinnamon
1 tablespoon lemon juice

Instructions
1. Put the carrots and onion in the slow cooker. Add the chicken, then the fruit.
2. Mix together the broth, tomato paste, spices, flour, and lemon juice. Pour over chicken and fruit.
3. Cook on low for 8 hours or on high for 4 hours.

Serves 4.

The pots, which were originally used as portable ovens by traveling Berbers, are glazed clay vessels with heavy round bases and cone-shaped lids. The shape of the vessels retains heat and traps steam, which keeps what is being cooked inside the pots from drying out. And that could be almost anything.

There are countless varieties of tagines. Most contain a mix of sweet and savory ingredients, a flavor combination that the Arabs brought to Morocco. One of the most popular tagines features chicken, olives, preserved lemons, saffron, ginger, and garlic. Other tagines combine different vegetables, dried fruit, nuts, and spices. Still others feature lamb, dried fruit, honey, ras-el-hanut, and olive oil. Originally, the Berbers were more likely to use butter in their recipes, but Spanish and Moorish influences made olive oil popular.

No matter the ingredients, all tagines are cooked slowly over low heat. This allows the liquid to thicken and become syrupy, the flavors to blend, and the meat and vegetables to become pull-apart tender. According to Wolfret, "After hours of slow simmering the meat comes out buttery and soft, and the sauce is full of spicy flavor."[6]

A Flaky Pie

Bastilla is another delicious Moroccan dish loaded with delicious ingredients and interesting flavors. It combines ingredients and cooking styles of the different groups that are part of Moroccan history.

Bastilla is a savory pie filled with alternating layers of shredded pigeon or chicken, scrambled eggs, and almonds. The pigeon or chicken is cooked in a rich sauce made with butter, onions, ras-el-hanut, and ginger. The eggs are cooked in lemon sauce and the almonds are coated with sugar. Each layer is topped with transparent, tissue-thin sheets of dough known as **warka** (war-ka), which, according to Wolfret, is: "the finest, thinnest, flakiest pastry in the world."[7] The final layer is

Bastilla is a flaky pie made of over a hundred layers of pastry and filled with anything from pigeon to eggs.

Muslim Dietary Rules

Most Moroccans are Muslim. They follow dietary rules set down by the **Koran,** their holy book. Acceptable food is said to be **halal**, which means lawful. Unacceptable foods are said to be **haram,** or forbidden. Haram foods include pork and pork products such as gelatin, animal blood, the meat of carnivores (e.g., dogs, wolves, rats, lions, and bears), birds of prey such as eagles, and land animals without external ears such as snakes. Eating the meat of animals offered in religious sacrifice or those killed by other animals, beating, strangulation, or by accident also is not permitted. Alcoholic beverages are also forbidden.

To be halal, animals must be slaughtered in a way that causes it the least pain. This involves quickly cutting the major arteries in the animal's throat, which drains all the blood out of its body.

crowned with sugar and cinnamon.

Because warka is extremely thin, it is difficult to make and work with. Moreover, a single pie can have one hundred layers of the pastry. Cooks who specialize in making bastilla often do so for a fee for others. And, ready-made warka is sold in Moroccan markets. Even so, preparing the pie can take hours, which may be why it is almost always served for special occasions.

No one knows the exact origins of the pie. The Berbers made a chicken dish similar to the poultry layer. The Arabs made a thinly stretched pastry, and the Moors learned to make savory pies in Spain. "One way or another," Hanger says, "it is a dish that illustrates the meeting of many cultures in its flavors."[8]

Unique Salads

Moroccan salads, too, mirror the nation's history and culture. For instance, salads that feature bulgur, a type of cracked wheat, originated with the Berbers. Sweet and savory salads were introduced by the Arabs, whereas those that feature tomatoes and peppers arrived by way of Spain. Uncooked green salads are a French contribution.

Moroccan salads come in a variety of combinations. They can contain hot and cold meat, vegetables, fruit, and nuts. Grated beets with lemon juice and parsley, eggplant stuffed with breadcrumbs and spices, bulgur surrounded by cooked vegetables, orange slices sprinkled with dates and almonds, or black olives and garlic, and chopped lamb's liver cooked in spices are just a few of the many interesting combinations. Almost every Moroccan meal is accompanied by several salads. In fact, it is not unusual for a dozen salads to be served. Travel Channel host, Andrew Zimmern described this array of salads as a "huge fanfare of food."[9]

Whether it's a variety of salads, multi-layered bastilla, diverse tagines, or couscous topped with dozens of different sauces, the Moroccan people enjoy a wide array of delicious foods. Each reflects the nation's rich history and culture.

Chapter 3

Sweet and Savory Snacks

Moroccans like to snack on both sweet and savory treats. Mint tea, delicious pastries, and grilled meats are popular specialties.

Sweet Mint Tea

In Morocco, mint tea is a symbol of friendship and hospitality. It is served before and after meals. Guests are given three glasses of tea, each a bit stronger than the last. Business transactions are conducted over tea. Shopkeepers offer tea to their customers. And it is a favorite treat at little cafes where Moroccans gather to visit and sip the refreshing beverage. Mustafa Yacine, a Moroccan man explains: "Everywhere you go in Morocco, the first thing they offer you is tea. It's an

Mint tea, a symbol of hospitality, is served before and after meals. Pouring the tea with the pot raised lets air mix with the tea. This causes foam to form on the top of each glass.

aperitif [appetite stimulant] before lunch and also it's a digestif [an aid to digestion] after lunch or after dinner. So you start with tea and you finish your dinner or food with tea, and while you're waiting for food they offer you tea—so mint tea, mint tea, mint tea, mint tea. Mint tea is something important in Morocco—it's the traditional drink...its something the Moroccans they can't pass [up]."[10]

Moroccans had their first taste of tea around 1880, when British traders brought it to Morocco from India. It soon became the Moroccan people's favorite drink.

Mint Tea

Fresh mint tea is delicious and simple to make. It is best to use fresh mint, but dried mint can be substituted. Moroccans like very sweet tea. Use less sugar for less sweet tea.

Ingredients
4 cups boiling water
4 teaspoons green tea
3 tablespoons sugar
1 bunch mint, about 1 ounce

Instructions
1. Put the tea, sugar, and mint in a teapot.
2. Pour in the boiling water. Stir well.
3. Let the tea steep for 3–5 minutes.
4. Pour the tea through a tea strainer into heat resistant glasses or cups.
Serves 4.

Moroccan Riads

Moroccan **riads** are large homes similar to villas or castles. Many are very old, whereas some have been built more recently. All riads are built around an interior courtyard, which provides privacy from the street. Orange and lemon trees are often planted in the courtyard, and there is usually a beautiful fountain. Balconies opening into the home surround the courtyard.

Most riads have thick walls made of mud, which keep the home cool. The walls of the courtyard and the inside of the home are usually decorated with a mosaic of beautiful handmade tiles. The tiles have intricate and colorful patterns and are famous throughout the world.

The floors are covered with handmade Moroccan rugs. There are thick cushions and plush sofas for relaxing. Beautiful brass lanterns made with stained glass hang from the ceilings.

Visitors to Morocco can stay in riads that have been turned into hotels.

Riads are large homes similar to villas or castles and are always built around an interior courtyard, which provides privacy from the street.

Moroccans prefer green tea flavored with lots of sugar and freshly picked spearmint. To ensure that the mint is fresh, farmers haul piles of mint on donkeys to the souks every morning. Many Moroccans grow their own mint in flowerpots. That way they can pluck fresh leaves off the plants whenever they want tea.

Moroccans are not only particular about what goes in their tea, they expect it to be prepared and served in a specific manner. First they pour boiling water into a tall thin brass or silver teapot perched on a gleaming metal tray beside three shiny little boxes containing tea, mint, and sugar. Then they add the ingredients to the pot, stir, and let it steep. Finally, the man of the house stands up, lifts the teapot high in the air, and pours the tea into little glasses on the table below. Pouring the tea in this manner lets air mix with the tea. This causes foam to form on the top of each glass. The tea is frothy, fragrant, and sweet. According to author Jessica B. Harris, it "appeals to all the senses. The eyes are gladdened by the amber hue of the tea; the nose twitches with the smell of the mint; the hand is warmed by the heat of the tea; and the mouth savors the taste. The ears? Well, when tea is traditionally served, the server pours a stream of tea into the glass from a teapot held aloft and the ears are delighted by the sound."[11]

Delightful Pastries

Pastries are a perfect accompaniment to mint tea. They are also frequently served at the beginning of a meal, rather than for dessert. Moroccans have many delicious pastries to choose from. **Kab el Ghzal** (kab-al-ha-zel), or gazelle horns, are among the most popular. Named for their shape, these long crescent-shaped pastries are made of thin flaky dough, filled with almond paste.

Kab el Ghzal, or gazelle horns, are among the most popular of Moroccan treats. These long crescent-shaped pastries are made of thin flaky dough, filled with almond paste.

Almond paste is a popular pastry filling in Morocco. It is made with ground almonds, butter, eggs, cinnamon, sugar, and water into which either rose petals or orange blossoms have been added. The addition of the flowers adds an exotic fragrance and flavor to the pastry, which is incredibly sweet and light. "I like the horns of the gazelle," explains Moroccan cook and blogger Sousou. "They are one of my favorite Moroccan cookies. They have a light texture, the dough layer is so thin that we almost don't feel its presence in our mouth."[12]

Mhencha (ma-hen-sha), or the snake, is another popular pastry with thin light dough. It, too, is named for its shape. Mhencha is a long coil of warka dough,

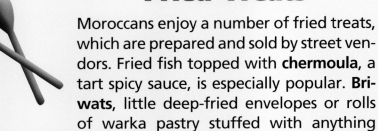

Fried Treats

Moroccans enjoy a number of fried treats, which are prepared and sold by street vendors. Fried fish topped with **chermoula**, a tart spicy sauce, is especially popular. **Briwats**, little deep-fried envelopes or rolls of warka pastry stuffed with anything and everything, are another favorite. Briwats can be sweet or savory depending on the filling. Popular fillings include chicken and onions, cheese and olives, almond paste, dates, or ground meat mixed with onions, cinnamon, and spices. Sweet briwats are topped with syrup.

Sfenj, or Moroccan doughnuts, are another fried treat. These pastries are not very sweet. Moroccans dust them with sugar and eat them warm with tea or for breakfast. They are often displayed and sold strung together like a necklace on a piece of cord.

filled with almond paste, then wrapped around and around itself, forming a circle of about 14 inches (35.5 cm) in diameter that resembles a sleeping snake. The giant pastry, which is topped with powdered sugar and cinnamon, is quite a sight. According to Roden, "It is stunning to look at and exquisite to eat."[13]

Other favorite pastries are less rich. **Fekkas** (fik-kas) are among this group. Fekkas look and taste more like crackers than they do cookies. They are made with flour, salt, sugar, butter, sesame seeds, anise seeds, almonds, and raisins. The dough is rolled into a log and partially baked, then left overnight to harden. The next day, the log is thinly sliced and baked again. The second baking takes the moisture out of the dough. The result is dry, hard, crunchy, slightly sweet cookies with a licorice-like flavor. Their texture makes them perfect for dunking in tea, which is what Moroccans like to do. "They are tough little things with a good taste," says Wolfret. "They are very popular for tea dunking, doubtless because they can stand the heat!"[14]

Grilled Meat

Savory snacks are also popular. Street vendors on the side of roads, in souks, and in town squares tempt hungry passersby with **kebabs** (kah-bahbs), grilled meat threaded through skewers and cooked over a charcoal fire. Kebabs are also the specialty of little eateries attached to butcher shops where customers purchase fresh meat, which they take next door to be cooked. As the customer watches, the chef, who is usually a member of the butcher's family, grills the meat and serves it with hot bread, which is made in the restaurant or in a neighboring bakery. Lisa Butterworth ("Kenzi"), an American who lived in Morocco, explains: "It's a simple meal but the ingredients are incredibly fresh, cooked in front of you, and served with bread that was made within feet of where you are sitting."[15]

No one knows where kebabs, which are also known as brochettes in Morocco, originated. Many nations take credit for them. It is known that Moroccans have been eating grilled meat cooked on a stick for centuries. Their favorite meat is lamb, which is cut into chunks and **marinated** in a tasty mix of olive oil, lemon juice,

Lamb kebabs are a traditional snack in Morocco, and its people have been eating them for centuries.

cinnamon, hot pepper, and other spices. Or the meat may be ground up, mixed with onions and spices, and molded into the shape of a sausage.

When the meat is ready for cooking, it is threaded onto a thin metal skewer. Pieces of lamb fat taken from the animal's tail are placed on the skewer, too. As the meat cooks, the fat drips onto the meat, moistening it, while the smoke and charcoal scent it.

When the meat is brown on the outside and juicy on the inside, it is removed from the skewer and wrapped in a piece of fresh hot Moroccan bread. Hot sauce, known as harissa (ha-ree-sa), is sprinkled on top of the meat along with salt and cumin. Salad and fried potatoes usually accompany the kebab, and are frequently

Lamb Kebabs

Kebabs are not difficult to make. Beef can be substituted for lamb.

Ingredients
1 pound lamb, cut into 2-inch (5-cm) cubes
½ cup olive oil
½ cup lemon juice
½ teaspoon cinnamon
½ teaspoon sugar
1 teaspoon crushed red pepper
salt to taste

Instructions
1. Combine the lemon juice, olive oil, cinnamon, crushed red pepper, and salt in a bowl.
2. Marinate the meat in the mix for at least one hour.
3. Thread the meat onto the skewers.
4. Grill the meat on a grill or in a broiler. Let the meat brown on one side then turn the skewer over. The meat is done when it is brown on both sides.
5. Remove meat from the skewers before serving. Serve with hot bread.
Serves 4.

piled right onto the bread. The result is a warm, spicy, and delicious sandwich.

Snacks like juicy kebabs, sweet hot mint tea, delicate pastries filled with almond paste, and crunchy anise-flavored cookies are delicious treats. They are but a few of the sweet and savory snacks available to hungry Moroccans.

Chapter 4

A Time for Sharing

Generosity and hospitality is an important part of Moroccan culture. It is unthinkable for a guest to leave a Moroccan home hungry. Holidays and special occasions give Moroccans a chance to share special foods.

Fasting and Feasting

Nearly all Moroccans are Muslim. Most Moroccan holidays are tied to religious holy days. **Ramadan**, a month-long religious holiday that falls at different times each year, is an important time of the year in Morocco. During Ramadan, Muslims typically **fast** from dawn to dusk in an effort to purify their souls. This means skipping food and drink during the day. Daily meals are

Muslim women enter a mosque in Casablanca, Morocco. Nearly all of the country's people are Muslim, and holidays are tied to religion.

limited to two: suhoor (so-hoor), a pre-dawn meal that starts the daily fast, and iftar (if-tar), the evening meal that breaks it. Moroccans eat liberally at both meals.

Iftar, in particular, is a festive meal in which special foods are served. Every day during Ramadan, the breaking of the fast and the start of iftar is announced by the firing of cannons throughout Morocco. At the sound, Moroccans crowd the roads, hurrying home for iftar.

Iftar gatherings usually involve many people. According to Muslim tradition, no one is supposed to eat iftar alone. Throughout the month, Moroccans warmly

Moroccan Banquets

Moroccans often celebrate weddings and other festive occasions with lavish banquets or **diffas**, designed to showcase the host's hospitality. Huge amounts of food are served at a diffa. There are usually anywhere from six to twenty courses. The first course is almost always bastilla. Next come different tagines, soups, salads, and bread. The final course is a heaping mound of couscous. It is followed by dessert and mint tea.

Women cooks are often hired to prepare all the food. Many of these cooks are the ancestors of black slaves who were brought to Morocco from the Sudan in the seventeenth century. The cooks shop, cook, and prepare all the food for the banquet. Some of these women also work in Morocco's finest restaurants and hotels and are famous chefs in Morocco.

welcome family, friends, neighbors, and even strangers into their homes to share the meal. "We have something called a 'darah,'" Leila Hazmi, a Moroccan homemaker, explains. "The word is derived from the Arabic word for circle or cycle and we use the word to describe the visits and family gatherings which take place during the month. Things happen in a rotating way, with everyone taking turns being guest and host."[16]

The Iftar Meal

Many different foods are served for iftar. Although menus vary, the fast is almost always broken with dates. This tradition began in the 7th century when Islam's prophet Mohammed broke his daily fast with the sweet fruit. Dates may be eaten plain, with milk, or stuffed with almond paste.

The rest of the meal is served all at once. Pastries, soups, meats, salads, tagines, all are placed in the center of the table for diners to eat in any order they prefer. "People…begin eating immediately and eat everything at one time. In fact, everything is placed on the iftar table even desserts,"[17] Leila explains.

Harira (ha-ria), a rich velvety soup, is usually among these dishes. In fact, many Moroccans eat it at every iftar meal. There are hundreds of different versions of the soup. Every cook has his or her own recipe. Typically, it contains crushed or **pureed** chickpeas and/or lentils, bits of meat, vegetables, tomatoes, tiny noodles, and lots of herbs and spices. Some cooks add a beaten egg mixed with lemon juice, which thickens the soup

Harira soup is served with nearly every iftar meal. It is a velvety soup that contains crushed or pureed chickpeas and/or lentils, bits of meat, vegetables, tomatoes, tiny noodles, and lots of herbs and spices.

and gives it a lemony scent and flavor. Others serve lemon slices on the side and add a little flour to thicken the soup. In Morocco's royal court, eggs are often soft boiled in the soup, then removed and served separately in little silver cups. Christine Benlafquih who lives in Morocco explains: "Recipes vary greatly from one family to another. Some make the soup light in texture; others prefer a filling version with chickpeas and rice or broken vermicelli [a type of pasta]. One Moroccan cook may favor more tomatoes, another more lentils, still another may add paprika....No matter what the family prefers, almost all choose to thicken harira's rich broth with either eggs or flour."[18]

Chebakia, a fried pastry similar to a doughnut, is usually made in large batches at the start of Ramadan.

Although North Americans might eat salty crackers with soup, Moroccans prefer sweet pastries. Honey-coated pastries known as **chebakia** (she-bek-ee-ah) are especially popular. Moroccans like mixing sweet and spicy flavors, and eating sweet chebakia with spicy harira does just that.

Chebakia is a fried pastry similar to a doughnut. The dough, which is made with yeast spiced with anise, cinnamon, and saffron, is either squeezed through a pastry tube in the shape of a flower, or folded and twisted by hand into a flower-like shape. Next, it is deep fried until it is golden brown. Then, it is immediately soaked in hot honey and sprinkled with sesame seeds.

Making chebakia is complicated and takes at least two people—one to fry the pastries and another to dip them. It is not unusual for family members or neighbors to get together to make the pastries, especially because Moroccans usually make huge batches of chebakia at the start of Ramadan. That way, they have enough to share with iftar guests for the whole month. According to Wolfret, "In a Moroccan home it wouldn't make sense to make less than five hundred cakes. Friends and neighbors help, and then everyone goes home with a large batch."[19]

During Ramadan, street vendors also sell chebakia. Cooks in Moroccan cafes and restaurants, which are

Carrot Salad

Moroccans serve many hot and cold salads with each meal. This makes an excellent salad or side dish. It can also be made with raw shredded carrots.

Ingredients
1 pound baby carrots, cut in halves
¼ cup extra virgin olive oil
3 tablespoons lemon juice
¼ cup chopped parsley
½ teaspoon garlic powder
¼ teaspoon cumin
¼ teaspoon cinnamon
¼ teaspoon sweet paprika
pinch of salt

Instructions
1. Fill a saucepan with water. Add carrots. Bring to a boil over medium-low heat. Cook the carrots 5–10 minutes until they are tender but not mushy.
2. Drain the carrots. Add the parsley.
3. Combine all the other ingredients. Mix well. Pour over the carrots. Toss gently.

Serves 4.

Safe Drinking Water

Eighty-two percent of Moroccans have access to clean drinking water. Either it is piped into their homes, they have a private well, or they have access to a public tap or well. Eighteen percent of Moroccans do not have easy access to clean water. Most of these people live in rural villages located in Morocco's Atlas Mountains. Girls and women in these villages travel miles to rivers or springs to get water, which they then haul home on donkeys. This water is not always clean and may carry waterborne diseases, which is one reason why the infant mortality rate in these villages is four times Morocco's national average.

Currently, the Moroccan government and a number of international organizations are working to bring water from mountain springs to reservoirs that are being built above these villages. Here, the water will be purified and piped into the villages.

Moroccans living in the mountains often have to walk miles to a spring where they haul clean water back to their homes on donkeys.

closed between sunrise and sunset during Ramadan, spend the day making chebakia and other pastries for Moroccans to buy after the cannons are sounded. The pastries are piled high on tables. Moroccans buy so many at a time that sellers provide pails to carry the pastries.

The Feast of the Sacrifice

The **Feast of the Sacrifice** is another festive and important religious holiday in Morocco. This three-day-long holiday celebrates the end of the Islamic year and the Biblical story in which Abraham agreed to sacrifice his son to prove his faith. At the last moment the boy is spared. In gratitude, Abraham sacrifices a lamb. In remembrance of the event, lambs are slaughtered and eaten all over Morocco.

During the week before the holiday, farmers and shepherds bring millions of live lambs to Moroccan cities and towns. About five million are sold for the holiday. Every family buys at least one lamb, and most buy more. Moroccans save up all year for the lambs, just as many people in North America save up for Christmas. Moroccans take the animals to their homes, where they keep them in gardens, courtyards, and kitchens. The animals are fed well and adorned with henna, a natural red dye.

On the first morning of the Feast of the Sacrifice, the men of the house slaughter the lambs in a humane manner prescribed by the Muslim religion as the whole family watches. Traveling butchers go from

A week before Feast of the Sacrifice, a family will buy a lamb and care for it in their garden or courtyard at home. On the last day, the lamb is slaughtered as prescribed in the Muslim religion.

Stuffed Dates

Dates are sweet, delicious, and nutritious. Stuffed dates make a good dessert, snack, or special treat. Ground almonds may be purchased in some grocery stores, or whole or slivered almonds can be ground in a food processor.

Ingredients
20 dates
1 cup sugar
1 cup ground almonds
1 teaspoon lemon juice
2 tablespoons water

Instructions
1. Cut a lengthwise slit down the center of each date without cutting through or cutting into the ends. Remove the seeds.
2. Mix the almonds, sugar, water, lemon juice together to form a firm paste.
3. Stuff about a teaspoon full of almond paste into each date. Press the paste in.

Makes 20 stuffed dates.

house to house to assist. Brahim Benhim, a Moroccan man, recalls: "I remember as a child my father used to help slaughter sheep for the elderly or neighbors who couldn't do it. He even had to travel to Saleh, which is another city across the river…help them out and then come back home and do ours last."[20]

Once the animals are slaughtered, at least one-third of the meat is given away to the poor. Fatima Baraka, a Moroccan woman explains: "It's a time for giving, remembering the poor and those who have less than you....I think the giving of alms [charity] and the sharing of food...is a very peaceful thing. It is a very nurturing thing, it's something that is necessary in our lives."[21]

The rest of the meat is turned into hundreds of delicious dishes, which are eaten over the next three days. Whole lambs are rubbed with spices, stuffed (with dates, almonds, and honey), put on a spit, and slowly roasted over a pit filled with hot coals. Chunks of meat are used in tagines, couscous, soups, and kebabs. And no part of the lamb is wasted. Lamb heart and liver kebabs are quite popular. The animal's head is steamed with spices. Even the eyeballs are eaten. Although this might not sound appetizing to everyone, the practice is part of Moroccan culture and tradition, as is eating and sharing special food with family, friends, and those in need. Holidays such as Ramadan and Feast of the Sacrifice give Moroccans an opportunity to open their homes and their hearts to each other.

Metric Conversions

Mass (weight)

1 ounce (oz.)	= 28.0 grams (g)
8 ounces	= 227.0 grams
1 pound (lb.) or 16 ounces	= 0.45 kilograms (kg)
2.2 pounds	= 1.0 kilogram

Liquid Volume

1 teaspoon (tsp.)	= 5.0 milliliters (ml)
1 tablespoon (tbsp.)	= 15.0 milliliters
1 fluid ounce (oz.)	= 30.0 milliliters
1 cup (c.)	= 240 milliliters
1 pint (pt.)	= 480 milliliters
1 quart (qt.)	= 0.96 liters (l)
1 gallon (gal.)	= 3.84 liters

Pan Sizes

8-inch cake pan	= 20 x 4-centimeter cake pan
9-inch cake pan	= 23 x 3.5-centimeter cake pan
11 x 7-inch baking pan	= 28 x 18-centimeter baking pan
13 x 9-inch baking pan	= 32.5 x 23-centimeter baking pan
9 x 5-inch loaf pan	= 23 x 13-centimeter loaf pan
2-quart casserole	= 2-liter casserole

Temperature

212°F	= 100°C (boiling point of water)
225°F	= 110°C
250°F	= 120°C
275°F	= 135°C
300°F	= 150°C
325°F	= 160°C
350°F	= 180°C
375°F	= 190°C
400°F	= 200°C

Length

1/4 inch (in.)	= 0.6 centimeters (cm)
1/2 inch	= 1.25 centimeters
1 inch	= 2.5 centimeters

Notes

Chapter 1: Bright Colors, Enticing Aromas, and Unique Flavors

1. Claudia Roden. *Arabesque: A Taste of Morocco, Turkey, & Lebanon.* New York: Alfred Knopf, 2009, p. 20.

2. Catherine Hanger. *World Food: Morocco.* Victoria, Australia: Lonely Planet, 2000, p. 30.

3. Paula Wolfret. *Couscous and Other Good Food from Morocco.* New York: Harper and Row, 1973, p. 30.

4. Catherine Hanger. *World Food: Morocco*, p. 46.

Chapter 2: A Cultural Blend

5. Lahcen Beqqi. "The Art of Moroccan Cuisine." *Lahcen's Moroccan Cooking.* http://fescooking.com/the-art-of-moroccan-cuisine.

6. Paula Wolfret. *Couscous and Other Good Food from Morocco*, p. 265.

7. Paula Wolfret. *Couscous and Other Good Food from Morocco*, p. 2.

8. Catherine Hanger. *World Food: Morocco*, p. 54.

9. Quoted in Shannon Demers. "Andrew Zimmern Bizarre Foods: Morocco." *The Travel Channel.* Executive producer Colleen Needles Stewart, aired March 5, 2007.

Chapter 3: Sweet and Savory Snacks

10. Quoted in Encounter. "Morocco and the Feast of the Sacrifice." *Radio National*, Transcript, July 14, 2002. www.abc.net.au/rn/relig/enc/stories/s603432.htm.

11. Jessica B. Harris. *The Africa Cookbook.* New York: Simon & Schuster, 1998, p. 340.

12. Sousoukitchen. "Horn of the Gazelle." September 19, 2009. http://sousoukitchen-en.over-blog.com/article-46926488.html.

13. Claudia Roden. *Arabesque*, p. 132.

14. Paula Wolfret. *Couscous and Other Good Food from Morocco,* p. 312.

15. Lisa Butterworth ("Kenzi"). "The Same Dirt That Grows Henna Also Grows Edibles." *Moor*, April 2010. http://moorhenna.wordpress.com/2010/04/.

Chapter 4: A Time for Sharing

16. Quoted in Somayya Jabarti. "Iftar—Different Cultures Have Different Dishes," *Arab News*, November 14, 2003. http://archive.arabnews.com/?page=9&section=0&article=35062&d=14&m=11&y=2003

17. Quoted in Somayya Jabarti. "Iftar."

18. Christine Benlafquih. "Moroccan Harira." *About.com.* http://moroccanfood.about.com/od/moroccanfood101/a/Harira_Soup.htm.

19. Paula Wolfret. *Couscous and Other Good Food from Morocco,* p. 303.

20. Quoted in "Morocco and the Feast of the Sacrifice." *Radio National,* www.abc.net.au/rn/relig/enc/stories/s603432.htm.

21. Quoted in "Morocco and the Feast of the Sacrifice."

Glossary

anise: An herb with a licorice-like flavor.

bastilla: Multi-layered chicken or pigeon pie.

Berbers: Nomadic African people who were Morocco's first settlers

chebakia: Fried pastry popular during Ramadan.

couscous: Pasta-like granules of semolina; often topped with sauce.

couscoussier: A pot used for making couscous.

fast: Willingly giving up food and drink for a period of time.

Feast of the Sacrifice: A festive Moroccan holiday in which lamb is eaten. It honors the biblical story in which Abraham offers to sacrifice his son to prove his faith.

fekkas: Twice-baked pastries similar to crackers.

harira: Lentil and tomato soup often eaten during Ramadan.

kab el Ghzal: Pastries filled with almond paste and shaped like gazelle horns.

kebab: Grilled meat threaded through a skewer, also known as a brochette.

marinated: Soaked in a sauce before cooking.

mhencha: Pastry shaped like a coiled snake.

Moors: Arabs who conquered Spain and later settled in Morocco.

puree: Grind solid food into a paste.

Ramadan: A month-long religious holiday in which Muslims fast from sunrise to sunset in an effort to purify their souls.

ras el hanout: A blend of many different spices.

semolina: Coarsely ground bits of wheat.

souks: Open-air markets laid out over many streets and alleys.

tagine: A clay pot with a conical lid; a stew made in this clay pot.

warka: Very thin pastry dough.

For Further Exploration

Books

Lynda Cohen Cassanos. *Morocco*. Broomall, Pennsylvania: Mason Crest, 2009. Discusses Morocco's geography, history, government, and people.

Sandra Donovan. *Teens in Morocco*. Mankato, Minnesota: Compass Point, 2008. Tells what life is like for young people in Morocco.

Dorothy Kavanaugh. *Morocco*. Broomall, Pennsylvania: Mason Crest, 2007. Focuses on Morocco's history and current issues facing the nation.

Websites

Central Intelligence Agency (www.cia.gov/library /publications/the-world-factbook/geos/mo.html). Information on Morocco's geography, government, economics, people, and military, including a map, flag, and photos.

Countries and Their Cultures (www.everyculture .com/wc/Mauritania-to-Nigeria/Moroccans.html). Information about life in Morocco including religion, education, home and family life, customs, holidays, and food with one recipe.

National Geographic Kids (http://travel
.nationalgeographic.com/travel/countries/morocco-
guide/). Gives fast facts, a map, flag, video, and many
photographs.

Index

M
Markets, open-air, *6,* 6–7, *11,* 11

Meals
  customs, 9, 19, 21
  salads, 27
Meat
  in bastillas, 24
  dietary rules, 20–21, 26
  kebabs, 35–38
  in tagines, 23–24
  See also Lamb
Mhencha, 33–34
Mint tea
  freshness of mint, 31–32
  importance, 28, 30
  pouring, 29, 32
  recipe, 30
Moors, 17
Morocco
  basic facts, 4, 7
  history, 17–18, 18
Muslim religion
  arrival in Morocco, 17
  dietary rules, 20–21, 26
  Sabbath, 21
  women entering mosque, 40
  See also Holidays

N
Number seven, 21

O
Olive and chickpeas recipe, 16
Olives, 14–16, *15*

Open-air markets, *6,* 6–7, *11,* 11

P
Pastries
  chebakia, 44–45, 45, 47
  fekkas, 34–35
  kab el Ghzal, 32–33, 33
  mhencha, 33—34
Pies, 24, *25,* 26–27
Pork, 20–21, 26
Pots, 19

R
Rabat, 7
Ramadan
  fasting, 39, 42
  hospitality, 42, 51
  See also Iftar meal
Ras el hanout, 9
Recipes
  carrot salad, 45
  chicken tagine, 23
  lamb kebabs, 37
  lemon cake, 13
  mint tea, 30
  olives and chickpeas, 16
  stuffed dates, 50
  sweet and spicy couscous, 20
Riads, 31

S
Saffron, 7–8, 44
Salads, 27, 45
Semolina, 9

Picture Credits

Cover Photo: © P. Desgrieux / photocuisine / Corbis.

AFP/Getty Images, 48-49

© Alistair Laming/Alamy, 11

© Bon Appetit/Alamy, 25, 33, 44

© Cephas Picture Library/Alamy, 8

© City Image/Alamy, 31

© imagebroker/Alamy, 22, 36

© Imagestate Media Partners Limited - Impact Photos/Alamy, 10

© Jim Wallace/Alamy, 40

© Laurie Strachan/Alamy, 12

© Lonely Planet Images/Alamy, 29

© Marck Eveleigh/Alamy, 46

© nobleIMAGES/Alamy, 6

© PBstock/Alamy, 18

© Photocuisine/Alamy, 21

© Simon Reddy/Alamy, 43

© Yvette Barnett/Alamy, 15

About the Author

Barbara Sheen is the author of more than sixty books for young people. She lives in New Mexico with her family. In her spare time, she likes to swim, walk, garden, and read. Of course, she loves to cook!